Oregon

Books by Henry Carlile

The Rough-Hewn Table
Running Lights
Rain

Oregon

poems by
Henry Carlile

Carnegie Mellon University Press
Pittsburgh 2013

Acknowledgments

Grateful acknowledgment is made to the editors and publishers of the following publications in which these poems first appeared:

Burnside Review: "Wide Heaven, the All-Sustaining Air"
Crazyhorse: "Oregon"
Cutbank: "Ashes"
Gray's Sporting Journal: "An Old Shirt of Raymond Carver's,"
    "Deschutes"
Oregon Literary Review: "Be Boppity Bop," "Burial at Sea," "Modern
    American Poetry"
Poetry: "Helium," "Mary," "Nature," "Ugly Money"
Tar River Poetry: "Dust"
The Southern Review: "Talk Show"
Willow Springs: "Andrew," "Davanti a la Ruina"

Thanks to the Oregon Arts Commission for their generous award of a grant that allowed me to complete several of these poems.

Special thanks also to Sandra McPherson for her responses to these poems in manuscript.

Book design: Nick Abele

Library of Congress Control Number 2012938305
ISBN 978-0-88748-560-2

10 9 8 7 6 5 4 3 2 1

for Genevieve

Contents

A Stray   9

Oregon   10

The Last DC-3   15

Uncle Andrew, December 1944   16

Andrew   17

Mother at Nineteen   19

Wide Heaven, the All Sustaining Air   21

Be Boppity Bop   23

Modern American Poetry   26

Ugly Money   28

Davanti a la Ruina   29

Three Haikus for a Bad Labrador   40

Ashes   41

Burial at Sea   45

Deschutes   47

An Old Shirt of Raymond Carver's   49

Catch and Release   50

Helium   52

Dust   53

Mary   55

Silver Thaw   56

Talk Show   58

"The Secret of Poetry is Cruelty"   59

First and Last   60

Nature   62

Ode to the John Day   64

A Stray

The dog that became so obstinately
yours after you explicitly told it not to
sits on its haunches outside your door,
wagging its tail. Tells you to let it in.
It does not whine or bark, it knows
what silences work best.
It will wait there all night or day.
Threaten it or try to ignore it, it will
not go away. And just when you think
it has finally got the message that
you can't be bothered, that you have
other, more amazing things to do,
and it is safe to open the door again,
it mysteriously reappears, always
glad to see you—the dog is patient.
It knows you better than you think,
loves to tear up things and eat paper.
Nothing is safe from its scrutiny.
It lifts its leg on your best intentions,
stubbornly deaf to all commands.
But should you follow as it snuffs
among the trash it treasures, who
knows what you might find? Do not
think of lost winning lottery tickets
or dead bodies. Think smaller than
that, the unspectacular space an ant
might occupy, where you can lose
yourself, at last, among the unregarded.

Oregon

Weeks pass this time of year without a glimpse
of sunlight, and a clammy, chilly dampness clings
to everything, wet rotting leaves, fog in the trees
through a dripping web of trunks and gray branches.
On the riverbanks the bleached, decaying carcasses
of the last spawned-out salmon, jaws sprung like
broken traps, and everything colorless, featureless
in the falling rain but the moss in visionary
shades of green, and the jade-gray papery lichen.
And on the topmost bare limb of the maple tree,
my black, iridescent friend, the crow, laughing.

Sometimes I long for a different landscape.
Not the dry desert of the Southwest, or the tropics—
those blonde beaches rife with escaping flesh—
but something plainer, flatter, clarified by
the chill of midwinter, smoke from chimneys
rising straight up into a blue sky,
remote farms scattered among fallow fields,
wind through wires, ice ticking against glass,
and everything sharpened to a promise
flamboyant as a cock pheasant in snow.
I know these are the tricks of elsewhere.
Once there, I would dream of bare wet branches,
plain dark bodies that one by one take the leaves'
places before they flutter off like leaves.

Each place has its beauty, unappreciated
until we lose it. Each person the same. We have
to dig to remember the unrest that brought us
to this state, for something resists

the emptiness we felt standing before a window,
looking out, or plodding head down through
rain puddles, through snow, recalling
conversations that never quite connected, alien
faces of the too familiar. Yet it all seemed
wonderful at first, the new life just beginning,
or else ending like a novel: *And so we think*
he drove off that morning knowing he was never
coming back. The sun was just topping the hill
as his truck cleared the front gate.

Simply clear out and never come back—that
is the hope, and yet we always do come back,
if not in flesh, in thought, and everything
is fixed forever as it was, though edited
by memory, that revisionist, that liar.
The empty spaces with their scatterings
of quaint houses, a church and small shops,
will never yield to shopping centers and avenues
of trash. And the inhabitants, sanctified by nostalgia,
will stay as we want them to, their petty slights
forgotten, for what is memory without amnesia,
that country of fog rising to meet the rain?

Sometimes I dread the thought of dying here,
in this place I have always dreamed of leaving,
until I realize that the place we dream of
will always be another we carry with us, not
the one we finally find ourselves in.
Old age, as Larkin said, *is having lighted rooms*
inside your head with people moving

and conversing, ghosts, the friends who died
or moved away, their letters fading,
their faces forgotten, nothing left but words,
So long, Good-bye, Take care—down corridors,
in airports, depots, before the last door closes.

I've always loved that rush down the runway
and the weightlessness as the wheels lift free,
the past falling behind, rain scribbled
by acceleration before the blank whiteness
that seems endless until it thins to blue,
the world's curvature carved by a silver wing,
time itself suspended as altitude slows us
to a crawl. Then it was only the new world
we were leaving that seemed old,
only future time we were flying toward, the sun
at our tail we hurried to meet in a new place,
a novel adventure we might never return from.
But home, like ocean, has its undertow.

When I was Catholic I wanted to sing in the choir
but had no voice; I wanted to be an angel, dreamed
of flying with arms that worked like wings; I emptied
a holy water fount and soused myself like a Baptist,
thinking to become a saint. The priest who caught me
must have thought me innocent enough. I never
waited to find out, but shot through the cathedral door
like a wet dog through a nimbus of waterdrops, the sin
of excess on me as I flew from the priest's laughter.
I would dream of the holy virgin opening her robes,
gathering me in, canonized, and wake to find myself

erect. Bernini understood the erotic in that mystery,
and St. John, with Christ's tongue stuck in his heart.
From treble to bass the choiring voices fell.

The morning my wife left I sat on the stairs and wept,
scared by the hurt animal sound of it. I wanted to stop.
There were shadows on the walls where paintings had hung,
blank spaces on the shelves her books had stood on,
no couch, no chairs, no table, no linen or bed.
When Ray came he said through a cloud of cigarette smoke,
This place looks like a house in one of my stories.
It feels like death. You've got to sell it.
He knew, he'd been there once.
Three years later he was dead and I'm still here,
my boat docked on its trailer, my rods racked and still
rigged with the last lures we used to fish the Strait.
Ray, this entire country begins to look like
a house in one of your stories.
In some trailerhouse of the spirit, at the dead end of
hope, a cigarette burns down in an ashtray
beside a half empty glass of whiskey,
as the TV with its twisted, foil-wrapped rabbit-
ear antenna shrieks—monster trucks leaping
the crushed chaos of Camaros and Impalas.
I haven't the saint's generosity, or Whitman's,
to call it beautiful, only the pure fear of death
instructs me to call it better than nothing,
to grind this butt in the ashes of grace.
You're gone, and so is Stafford, who loved this place,
a saintlier man than either of us, and Oregon persists
in being Oregon, God's country to those

who have never lived here or any place but here.
I haven't the arrogance to call this God's country.
Last night an earthquake rattled the windows,
the second this year, and the year barely begun.
Maybe it will shake some sense into us.
Maybe it will scare me into loving
what I've taken for granted.

Last fall I watched a single pair of salmon hovering
over a redd on a tailout that once held hundreds.
The male was hook-nosed and battered, charging
an enterprising trout on the prowl for eggs.
The female turned on her side, fanning away the silt
from the streambed with her frayed tail. All afternoon
I watched until their spawning began—
the female thrashing as she cast her burden
to the stream, the clean declivity where her eggs
could swirl and rest, and the male's great
shuddering spasm as he loosed his sperm and
the white flood swirled over the redd and clouded
the current downstream. They would spend
the short remainder of their lives guarding that spot.
I felt the terrible privilege of my place at the
river's edge, called to witness the end of something.
I wanted to put back every fish I had ever caught,
I wanted to beg forgiveness of everyone I'd hurt,
but the feeling passed. We learn remorse
by the feeblest fits and starts, we learn to love
when what we should have loved is lost.

The Last DC-3

Flying home that night on my first leave,
I remember how the long silver wings flexed
like a bird's in the moonlight as we bumped
through a patch of unstable air, and the glow
of the exhaust manifold in the starboard nacelle
was like a friendly stove, the deep vibration of
the propellers and moonlit mountains below,
our destination Moon Island Airport
in Hoquiam, with its mill smoke and rain.

And I wished a woman like Ingrid Bergman
might rise from her seat and float through
the rare air and ask me to light her cigarette.
But only the usual passengers were sleeping,
talking quietly, reading or smoking in the narrow
fuselage with seats two abreast on either side
and quaint curtains tied back from the windows.
I was nineteen years old, on my first flight ever,
fresh out of basic and safe from a war just ended.

Experienced pilots affectionately call it
"a collection of parts flying in loose formation."
By then it was obsolete, but still holding on,
seventeen hours coast to coast with three stops,
a "tail dragger" pointing its nose skyward even
at rest, as though it couldn't wait to get back into
its element—cold blue sky, cirrus clouds—barely
reaching the jet stream before they called it that.
But don't I know how silly it is to love a machine?

Uncle Andrew, December 1944

The inside of his tank was painted white, with only slits
to see through, a kind of solitary confinement, though
there were others, a commander, loader and gunner.
He was the driver. His last day in that white space
what did he think as he drove dipping and plunging
through the Ardennes, that the forest was not so beautiful?
Or that fog-shrouded snowy woods concealed German
Tigers and Panthers, *Panzerfausts*, *Nebelwerfers* and 88s,
that could crack his M5's armor like a walnut?
He was fresh from the States on his first engagement.

So it must have been a relief when at last they pulled him
off the line to refuel and take a break from fighting.
Outside, he would have felt free of a great weight,
gratefully drinking coffee from a canteen cup
and maybe thinking of his wife and children.
But others might have heard something like the wind
rising in the trees, and perhaps one or two shouted.
The one hit never hears it, but how would they know?
Then it was over—I can almost imagine it—
His helmet rolling and rolling like an empty shell.

Andrew

The German who killed my mother's youngest brother,
probably never knew he did it.
It was cold that day in the Ardennes, snow everywhere,
the forest shrouded in fog that hid their Panzers
from our grounded aircraft.
My uncle had been in action forty-eight hours without
a break, his tank out of ammo, almost out of fuel,
no match for the heavier armored Tigers patrolling
the main roads that had outflanked retreating
remnants of the Ninth Infantry's First Battalion.

Behind the lines, my uncle might have removed his helmet,
believing himself safe for awhile. He was drinking coffee.
From old news photos I have to recreate him
as he must have looked that day, the boyish stubble
on his face, the heavy circles beneath his eyes,
lifting the canteen cup half full and steaming in the bitter air.
The German was probably tired as my uncle,
maybe as young, with a wife and child like my uncle's
he would never return to. In that iron cold I have to
imagine him fumbling rounds into the mortar's muzzle,
trying to match the spotter's coordinates
somewhere beyond an intervening hill, a fringe of trees,
hearing between reports the distant heavy thud,
half muffled by snow, of his fatal handiwork.

I have to see his mittened hand sweeping in one
quick arc, the way it was drilled into him,
dumping the round in tail fins first, and hear it slide
down the tube and fire as he ducked and covered
an ear closest to the muzzle's blast.

I have to imagine the shape of the round at its apex,
turning over and starting its long demented plunge,
containing the fragment that would separate my uncle
from himself, the others already shouting and diving
for cover, and my uncle just standing there, lifting
the unholy aluminum grail of the canteen to his lips.
I remember Mother holding the telegram that morning
and crying my uncle's name, her voice so choked it seemed
at first she was saying, *And you! And you!*

Mother at Nineteen

At nineteen, could she have imagined herself
nineteen years later, helmeted and leathered,
holding a welding rod and wearing a necklace
of burn scars from the white-hot slag of her work?
This was her torch song arced out in the double
bottom of a Liberty ship, the long straight welds
like the seams she stitched with her Singer,
older than I am, that still runs, if I knew
how to make it work, to spin the bobbin winder
the way she did and thread the maze of loops,
hooks and wheels to the eye of the needle.

If I could figure out how to lock the stitches,
or fashion a button hole with the attachment,
maybe it would hum back those nights she
sewed and sang along with an old Philco
late into the night to barely earn our living,
making wedding gowns, uniforms
for the high school's drum majorettes, taking in
or letting out, tucking, pleating and mending,
altering the hemlines of women who looked
down on her as she knelt at their feet, a sliver
of chalk in her hand and her mouth full of pins.

In the cuttlefish-colored portrait in my study,
with her pageboy haircut, long string of beads
and Coco Chanel chemise, I could imagine her
wrecked on bathtub gin, dancing the Charleston
as I saw her once jitterbugging at a party
in the forties, but her eyes betray her,
looking askance of the camera, as though she

can't bear to see the life bearing down on her:
the long lines of unemployed that became
long lines joining up, the four she married
and three divorced, and her one child
a bedside stranger offering a bouquet of lilies.

Wide Heaven, the All Sustaining Air

In seventh grade she raised more than eyebrows,
Betty Lou with her black hair and dark eyes.
Jimmy Breedlove, especially, Breedy we called him,
stared as she crossed and uncrossed her legs and we
heard the faint electric crackle and hiss of her nylons,
she staring back at him, tonguing her upper lip
and watching the small, hard lump in his crotch rising
like the resurrection of the dead called home to Jesus,
smiling to herself as Miss Albrecht, rapping her ruler,
called on Breedy to stop his dreaming and stand
and deliver the "Charge of the Light Brigade,"
or the Twenty-Nine Articles, or the square root of n
to the tenth power divided by God knows what.

And he, book or paper held to screen his crotch,
weak eyes squinting behind horn-rimmed glasses,
would stammer his best response, while giggles
spread over the classroom, and Miss Albrecht
broke her ruler rapping for silence,
and Betty Lou, feigning innocence, her eyes cast
modestly down, pretended not to notice the fruits
of her effect on us, on poor Breedy in particular.

Betty Lou, the fastest girl in school, who at thirteen
partied and drank with high-school boys while we
desperately flogged ourselves behind locked doors of
bathrooms and bedrooms, imagining the slow removal
of her underthings, and collectively but separately
came deep into our adolescent fists, and shamed,
flushed the evidence of her power over us down drains
that emptied unfiltered to the river, a place where carp,

their fat, penny-copper scales reflecting dully,
jostled and gulped and multiplied on our city's effluvia.
Betty Lou, who wound up in reform school, last I heard,
for stabbing a man in the face with a broken bottle,
a bastard who probably deserved it.
Only in dreams could we beat her alcoholic father
off of her and kiss the bruises from her flesh.

Be Boppity Bop

Thelonious Monk, his tonsure his hat,
I love to hear him play, fingers strafing
the keys, whimsical, unpredictable.
Come back, clef caught in the halo
of her hair, black sign lost in white space.
Give back the sounds we never imagined,
so we can never forget the way she looked
bent toward him that way, love in her eyes,
love in her eyes and the lights turned low.
The bass picks up where being begins
and swings the drums along. I haven't felt
this way for a long, long while, she sings alone
in the shower, but here's where the blues start
on a rainy autumn night, the oldest and saddest
song, lost innocence and a broken heart.

And Miles asks, Why clutter it up? A dot here,
a sudden dash there, some strange new code.
rice paper splashed with ink.
We ought to think with our bodies
and park our shoes on the doorstep.
We need to be barefoot to feel the blues.
It's the phrasing again, the spaces around
words, around notes, the sound
of one hand suspended over the keys.
I saw the wooden door shut twice
inside the wooden face before the eyes
lit up and gave the face away.

Lady Day, Lady Day, we miss you
sounding off for all you're worth,

lamenting the lot of every woman.
What can we do, whatever do,
when the world goes wrong?

And when the music died.
I took the train down south
to practice other sounds:
the snap of tracers burning the air,
the same pollution everywhere,
falling in, falling out, endless shouting
yard to yard through the burned-out
barracks of human wrong.
What could I do but turn again to song?

We pound the tusks or pluck the gut
to tease the venom out,
because the tortured, beautiful notes
won't leave us alone.
Whoever asks, say we couldn't wait
but left these maps behind that they might,
tracing paths we took, discover others—
imitation, then innovation, riffing,
leap-frogging in fours, kneading the notes
into new surprising forms, jamming
after hours for the pure joy of it
until uncool dawn horns in with
its tiresome, usual commerce.

Love itself is rare enough you have
to treasure it until it goes.
That's when the blues begin.

You feel them like a woman
alone with midnight smoking in
the shadows between two lights.

God bless my stubborn heart, I believe
I saw her in the epistrophal dawn
like a note hanging from a stave,
pure essence of love, pure essence
beyond my wordy reach,
though I have spent my life trying,
believing in love's healing voice,
the glorious sounds from the garden
where the enraptured bird sings.

Modern American Poetry

Smoking a fat dark cigar and
reading us Wallace Stevens
he leaned toward the sorority
girl who had wrinkled her
nose, and asked, "Does this
lay an egg for you, Honey?"

And when she answered, "It's all
these cutesy little words he uses,"
Roethke tipped back, shrugged,
and said, "That's it in a pig's eye,"
and exhaled a perfect zero that
floated its judgment above us.

Most of us were shocked, and one
or two nervously giggled, but
in the years since, I've sometimes
wondered if Roethke ever guessed
that the Stevens he loved
never liked his poetry that much.

In a National Book Award
committee meeting Stevens once
asked, "Who's the coon?" pointing
at a photo of Gwendolyn Brooks.
Stafford said you must change
your life, a line that also appears

in a sonnet of Rilke's, but it's clear
now, the road to hell being paved
with good intentions etc., that

some do well despite themselves,
and the undeserving still
might wink like stars above us.

Face it, what poetry makes happen
is sometimes catastrophic: that bird
lover who imported starlings and all
the other birds in Shakespeare's plays
and poems, how could he imagine
bird strikes on the yet-to-be invented?

When Williams warned us against
leaving what is badly written and
told us to watch carefully and erase,
he wasn't being precious; he knew
that a stray word like *launch*
for *lunch*, could destroy the world.

And what about Marianne Moore's
"I, too, dislike it"? She, too, had her
doubts. Still, given the alternatives,
and able to find a name for anything
but a failed Ford venture in tasteless
design, she gave her good life to poetry.

Three months before he died, Roethke
grabbed me and said, "My doc says
if I don't lay off the sauce I've got six
months to live," and a few beats later,
"Let's get a beer at the Blue Moon."
What could I do then but follow?

Ugly Money

(for a poet who called money an unfit subject for poetry)

Were it prettier he could save it.
But why bother with such lettuce?
All the same monotonous shade
of something dead.

And the faces uninteresting, not
one woman among them. What make
of this surreal pyramid, its eye
surveying the desert of finance.

He thought the long green was
where putts are made, not this
flaccid unfolding,
this dead skin sloughed off,
inflated, then flatulent
as it zips away.

Davanti a la Ruina
G.E.C. 1904-1996

Where the speechless arrive and are given names.
Where the names arrive and are given numbers.
Where the poor remain poor and the rich are
passed through a needle's eye and become the meek,
the sere, the spiritually emaciated wandering
insatiable obscenities tending the furnaces.
O blister of blazing goggles. O rash of the damned.

No one's come to instruct him or to delight
in the horror he suffers at each soul's expense.
He watches from the abutment, having earned
the best view of the undone misfortunate many,
one of the few privileged enough to visit here
and return on the evening's red-eye flight
like a tourist from a Third World country.

What he has seen he has seen and must say
and find no words for, this his penance,
a surfeit, a poverty flies buzz over,
a carrion endeavor wafting its own
reek through the smoking landfills and waste
incinerators, over the bricked repetitions of projects
reflecting last light from smoked windows.

Give him your hand so recently dead
your scent still haunts the hangers your clothes
depend from, instruct him in the voices you've come to.
Dear Loved One, Dear Ghost, tell him what to make of it,
give him a name to call it in your name or God's,
for His sake or yours. Give him a hand, like the one he
held in the minutes after you left, still hot with you.

God grant him a mate, she says, *to make his writing*
a hell of housework, let the vacuum inhale
his choicest thoughts, the mop expunge all trace of
inspiration and belief, what he has seen he must
say and find no words for in his penance. Yes, but
he's seen what he's seen and will say it where You
and he, like lovers whirled to perdition, contend.

God's Grand Mosaic erupts from the floor.
He agreed to Nothing until he saw it, a gaudy peasant-
pheasant jewelry everywhere he looks, its patterns
repeating yet changing constantly, no tinctures
luminous enough to serve it, or note to sound it from
his register's imperfect scale, no speech to name it,
least expected, to this silence of depleted souls.

Why choose a life other than he's lived?
Pleasure and pain recreate each other protesting
what they're not, how could they neglect him here?
All around, the plaintive flute notes of the damned:
those sure of everything but unwilling to bet,
hares' eyes in all the hedges, no drink, no coffee
or cigarettes, and still their suspicious lumps.

Little we can do without God's help,
and why do we call these disasters meaningless
when we've taken such pains and nearly
exhausted a dead language to name them?
Latinate invisible flowers—*death no problem*
to be solved but a mystery entered into—
some *moraliste's* antithesis.

Not his. He'd still like to know and come back
to talk about it. No Disneyland tunnel of light
and love, but the real thing, out past the suburbs,
the spectacular light shows, the staged retinal
disasters resolved into family reunions without
codicils and contests, standing around the Body
and Blood punchbowl, full of inebriate good will.

Say like some odd Murphy of the spirit he went
to Hell and back, he'd still be charged with it,
linguistically challenged, so to speak, to step up
to the rail and slam it down the gullet, hang it
by its heels and spank some breath into it. But here
they won't even clean your windshield before
they send you out with full tank and license to kill.

Between the tenements old forgotten laundry
hangs, releasing its ammoniac smell,
the senile reek of poverty and spiritual dis-
ease, far from where he broods above it all
screened and porched in Sandstone luxury.
One of these days, he thinks, he will slip out of it
unnoticed by the noisy world. And all he has left behind?

Must live as best it can beside his chair, his table and bed,
his tools and furnishings, sporting goods,
mementos and books, a few thousand words
in a world sche-ream-ing-full of words that will change
nothing, least of all the hearts of those they addressed:
bosses and workers, politicians and parents,
his friend's grandfather, shingle sawyer forty years,

who beat the odds and never lost a finger or lost
at cards either, drawing from the bottom of the stack,
taking three or four instead of two, easy
if you play with double decks and a wife half blind
from more than old age and poor eyesight.
And his own grandfather? Dead before he was born,
banned from his wife's bed, she fanatic, rebrided to God.

How do you redeem Chaos except by writing to it?
Otherwise shut up and let inhuman nature take its course.
Where to begin, since there is old guilt everywhere you
step, like dogshit on the rues of Paris, pretension rampant,
and all the bookstores musty with selfages, variations on
Plato, Nietzsche, Descartes and Marx (the brothers
preferable in their pantomimetics). And the universities?

As usual, full of it, of tenure-tracked appointees to careers
in obfuscation, raccoon redundancies, branch Derridians,
having flunked Auden's lesson of writing profoundly
in the light manner—*Lux sit sensorum.*
And the poets, likewise, cowled and howling from
their leafy altitudes, jostling one another for attention,
scream obscenities and hurl down shit,

certain of touching someone with offal paw prints.
Into this Pandemonium he steps, hauntingly presented
as Nothing Himself, and the monks lay down their dung
regarding form and content into the void of him—
a host of fireflies besieging the darkness, a seven-year
plague of cicadas obsessed with auditorture—
his absence and darkness absorb them all.

War is Hell! the general said. The same might be
said for poetry and the paths we take to avoid it, sir.
Insert your point into the neck of the oyster and
swallow whole pollution on the half shell, a bogus
aphrodisiac but a certain hallucinogen, sure
to make the walls scream graffiti. *I haven't
trailed it this far to back down now,* he thinks.

He follows like fog through a flock of burning sheep,
lured to the nether regions, the nexus
impenetrable unto himself: *Here I am!*
shouts down the stairs at a locked door cyclopsed
with a peephole and nozzled by a brass knocker.
I am! I am! cascading through the corridors,
grayest pigeon of a blind belief seeking its home.

He could be a television evangelist for all he knows,
a pacing confusion of chapter and verse, addressing
himself to a chapel of mirrors—Ciacco the glutton
with a leg of mutton. A few thousand others tiered
like a strip mine or mall etched into the slope
of a mountain, poisonous with alkali and sulfur.
In his Colorado, coyotes lope beside the runways.

But an Oregon malice of rain absorbs him, softening
the ground, swallowing trees and sloughing away
whole hillsides in a crush of mud, while rivers rise,
littered with debris—bottles and barrels, boats and
boat decks, chairs intact, a plastic Buddha smiling
serenely as it passes under the Hawthorne Bridge,
released from karma as a gardener's ornament.

Where he loiters in the vestibule, its opportune face
arrests him, serene in the suck and swirl,
missed by the evening news. And you, Muse,
misshapen vessel of contestable fortune, aid him.
Ha! bring a skillet instead of a pen, an apron in lieu
of paper, let him serve my example and put up
his other pretense, she says.

A fried egg stuttering in a puddle of grease,
a heap of laundry on the cellar steps, glassware
to be rinsed and polished, pots to be scrubbed,
diapers and formula, measles and mumps.
I tell you he was like any brat, but more colicky,
good only when he was sleeping or sick,
but he was mine, for better or worse.

Mother me out of here! wrote Roethke in a fit of fear,
in what Bishop called his *schizophrenic* mode.
and *Time* ranked him above Robert Lowell
and both beneath a treasury of others, dead.
He didn't think drink had unhinged so many,
uneasy with this newest revelation.
It won't fly: Roethke. Or scan: Bishop.

And John Logan: *Stop writing sonnets, for God's sake!*
So he adopts the seven-line stanza as a half measure,
a cardinal number connoting the seven stages of man,
good luck or bad, seven come eleven, seven card stud,
the Seven against Thebes, the Magnificent Seven,
the Seven Deadly Sins and the Seven Seas, and ends with
seventh chord progressions in a fit of blues.

When the ones in camouflage creep through his lines,
the ones like bark, like leaf-heaps or shucks, white
as snow or black as night, he feels the red dot wandering
over his body, the trigger's final squeeze, his chest
exposing its flower, red peony or tea rose,
to bagpipes of a citizen's militia, and remembers his own
march against government, chanting *Give peace a chance!*

So what if the longhaired ones today would've lynched
their look-alikes in the '60s, who cares? The serpent belches
swallowing itself, and thereby commends the end
being served, hooped to another millennium.
This dog he's walking pulls him down the road. He got
the teeth that gnaw the knuckles down, he got
the coat as black as night . . . .

So what if he passes out clichés like Confederate money?
Lost in speculation he wanders from market to market
looking for a bargain, a suit of clothes, good used shoes.
But his dog follows, queering the deal, everywhere he goes.
Alpha dog. His sole concern, a world safe for retrievers.
A world without money and plenty of bones—whole
cemeteries free for the digging, a California bone rush.

At age seven, through a fever, he heard the diagnosis,
German measles, and saw a cast-iron swastika
break through the wall and felt the covers weight him
in lead—it was 1941, the Nazi invasion of North Africa,
the papers and airwaves full of it, and later the tissue
and balsa Spitfire and ME-109 banked in currents
above his bed in slow-motion aerial combat.

No one was ever killed there, nothing was ever gained.
He saw the war end with sailors and shopgirls dancing
through the streets and felt a pang of regret, guilt
dragged like a bag of dead cats to the confessional,
and to commemorate peace, lit a firecracker that
made a neighbor, shell-shocked and wounded at Iwo,
dive beneath his bed and fetched his wife screaming.

Alpha Dog, the shameless retriever, shags it all back,
farts under the bed, dodging the mother's broom,
a dust mote of a dog who won't be caught by a straw,
or swept in a pan, he must be a phantom, he has no fleas.
During Mozart his gnawing rises to a crescendo,
his hindpaw jigs an allegro in perfect syncopation
to the six-eight strain. Certain, he composes himself.

But she has been writing doggerel again,
says *You're not the only poet in this family,*
didn't speak to him for two years
following his first book; then, monosyllabic
in the months that followed, phoned him
weekly with succinct plans, asking
Where can I get this published?

Alpha dog, stalking the Omega of his own tale,
shambles past the shopfronts pitching
their hopeful slogans, and sniffs their aromas,
connoisseur of pancakes and sausages,
toting a copy of Whitman written in invisible ink.
His pelt, an ocean tossing minute messages
from its ships, a plaintive, continuous SOS.

Meanwhile, alone in his study, he writes:
A nation of (supply . . .) becomes a national
(. . . missing word) for a manual
of do-it-yourself speeches, and thinks *Even I*
must earn a living and so stoop to this!
half aware as the ratchet clicks the black knight,
his sword erect, into the ready position.

Everything hangs on the missing note:
the clapper cocked ready to strike,
the revelers awaiting the ball's drop
to usher in the New Year, the first chime
wound in every carillon, on every tongue,
in every church and university across the land,
an oath that echoes from the grating's mouth.

As if a truck had backfired its perfect O of soot
or an owl had screeched from a chimney
its fiery, feathery word, hung in mid-hoot
over the Seventh Avenue knockoffs,
slightly less marginal than their mannequins.
Those who don't know speak of it, those who
know don't—heady stuff for TV evangelists.

She, ninety-two and dying, doesn't recognize him.
She saw the pretty red horses again this morning.
Yesterday, it was her husband who died six years ago.
In the city, there aren't any, he tells her.
Only Mustangs and Pintos and Colts, before
he sees the Japanese maples outside her window
flaming their red manes.

In Ketchikan, out berry picking before he was born,
she bouldered bears to keep them from
the choicest bushes—dust eruptions from those
roaring rugs—and all gave way, glad to be quit
of her five feet and avalanche of stone.
And later, beach combing, she fended off
a thousand pound sea lion with a sack of wood.

Now she drifts with the other biddies
in the old folks home, her mind half here, half
stuck in memories, like a Model T with busted axle.
They've ruined her hair, amputated the long tresses
still not completely white and permed it to a frizz.
I don't know you, don't know you, don't know you,
a woman in a bathrobe says to no one in particular.

The other, fixed and angry in her wheelchair, says
I don't know him either. The rest home, recently
inundated, still reeks of floodwater, and she,
back from the Red Cross shelter, can't forgive him—
never mind the mudslides and washed-out roads
that kept him away—battleship-gray, her eyes,
in his childhood, fearsome, the same now.

Seen again as he puts pen to paper, as if paper
itself could stare him into stone.
Please, he asks. *How must I honor you?*
She is dying and it's his fault. Unstoppable,
the black knight begins its march from a hundred
clockworks in as many towers, and all over
the bells commence their tolling.

Here in Hell they clank loudest, in the wake of
a great soul passing beyond their drowned reach.
Coordinates of her ashes' scattering three miles
off the coast, a small bronze plaque among the
others crowding the harbor's narrow entrance,
a legacy of legal documents, photographs, post-
mortem other mementos, her voice, the sea's.

Through water like creamed coffee he wades,
testing the shallows, the receding margins
away from the torrent her soul and the Buddha
have followed. The laundry's done, the lamb roast
from the freezer almost thawed. He's washed
and vacuumed and dusted and mopped,
and called the dog in for its supper.

Among the night sounds his ears are used to—
refrigerator hum, furnace starting in the basement,
rattle of registers, faucet dripping or clock's tick,
the dog is loudest, lapping water from its bowl—
gelup, gelop—at three a.m. echoing from the kitchen,
waking his wife as he pretends to sleep, the river
and where it might take him gone for the time being.

Three Haikus
for a
Bad Labrador

Farting and scratching
at once, my dog has
mastered the tremolo.

Like a trout rising to a fly
the dog snaps
at something singing by.

Now dog, lifting your leg,
look what you have done
to the beautiful snow!

Ashes

He lay asleep, mouth agape, a strand of drool
like an IV anchoring him to his pillow,
his heartbeat ticking the monitor
just days away from death,
my stepfather, foundered like one already gone
among the other geezers in the VA ward.

When the mortician phoned, my mother
said, *That's dirt, not him, throw it in the sea.*
No ceremony with relatives in black.
Only a word or two at the local VFW,
the Elks, the Eagles, maybe the Moose
(my stepfather joined everything),
fraternal wildlife facing their own extinction,
the fishing boat crossing the bar,
the deckhand holding the urn of ashes.

Released from the hospital two days
before he died, my stepfather shook
my hand: *Still strong as iron!* he said.
Sometimes I wake to feel the pressure
of that grip, the pain of it, like a trap
of absence that won't let go,
like the .22 he left me I could never
hit anything with, and his compass
pointing hopelessly the way he went.

A ruddy little man, a grand liar, embarrassed
when the townsfolk coerced him every
Christmas into playing their Santa Claus,
his *Ho Ho's* frightened the children who had

to be coaxed into his lap with bribes of candy.
Christmas eves he came home quarrelsome,
diagnosed a drunk by his doctor, a drunk,
as if the doctor wanted company.

His heart enlarged to embrace the world
he was leaving, his last year hooked
to an oxygen hose, his daily company
a neighbor's cat, a view from his lawn chair
facing the driveway. My mother found him
at dawn, dead as a fish, released from his line,
away from the current that troubled him:
Why are we bombing civilians? he asked,
angering the other vets, patriots to the man.

And if he lied his way through life, always the hero
of his own fictions, who's to say he was wrong?
In the brown-tone photos that outlive him
he appears the shortest and fattest, clearly
the loudest of the lot among the dead animals
and hunting pals he managed to outlast.
That accident on the ranch became
an ammunition dump explosion at Fort Knox.
Antlers sprouted tines, fish stretched.
Lost fights became brave victories,
the imagined history of his unmanageable life,
no weirder than my ex-wife's eccentric aunt's
whose tabby, trafficked flat beside the road,
became a *sail cat* propped in a crotch
of the cherry tree, a place-mat cat,

scenic from her kitchen window
in the autumn rainfall of fermented fruit.

In my favorite photo my stepfather
and his three brothers
strut in a buggy behind the barn,
four bottles of whisky tilted in a toast
hidden from their mother in the pantry
frowned away from where they clown.
The horse droops in its traces,
as if bored or bemused.

*

Each morning he brought my mother
a water glass half full of vodka topped
with orange juice, each morning
unscrewed the cap from a bottle
of bourbon and slugged it down.
Now my mother wanders the rest home
screaming about the *Holocaust*,
waving *important papers*,
delusional from alcohol and drugs.
They find her at dawn, in a fetal position,
her room torn apart, certain she's survived
a plane crash barely less catastrophic
than her life: runaway at twelve,
married at thirty, four husbands—one
wife-beating brute, one child molester,
two alcoholics—all dead.
And a slew of shit jobs ending in ess.

Sometimes she mistakes me
for her husband. *Randy?* she calls.
Randy? No, Mama, I tell her, *It's Henry.*
Randy's gone. Of course, he is! she says,
as if I've told her something wrong.
Nothing I say can make her life seem
meaningful or right or bring to justice all
the slights, real or imagined, that stalk her.
I nod my head and agree to her complaints,
right or wrong. No relative or neighbor's left
unvilified, no trespass unforgiven
in her diary of harm. The trouble is, she's right
half the time: her world is ugly,
the people bad enough to make you hang
your head for what the human race can be.
I'm afraid of it, she says. *Afraid of what?* I ask.
A stupid question she will not answer.

Now I've consigned her to my stepfather,
gulls, flailing their wings, trouble
the calm her ashes have fallen through.
What coordinates of empty space her smoke
inhabits are anyone's guess. Those of us
who still breathe inhale a part of her
with every breath we take, the lonely molecules
that were her oxygen before they became our fire.

Burial at Sea

No word can name this thing
I feel brooding over the Pacific
and these scattered remains:
my poor, dead mother,
the pale film of her ashes cast
overboard and drifting astern;
my stepfather whose name
I carry like a cloud of my birth-
father's unknowing; and last,
my uncle, feeble-minded and
adrift in Seattle streets before
they picked him up to lose him
again in some other home
for the homeless, then months
after my mother's death, found
me, sole survivor, to sign away
his morgued and frozen remains.

When my time comes will I be cast
with them or urned in the arms
of my loving wife, belled against
the rips they race through?
Beneath black polished granite,
my friend rests at a bluff's edge
that will someday crumble
to the same strait and salt rush
we fished together for salmon,
drawn by the moon's and heart's
gravities and stubborn pace.

I can't make sense of it:
the lights of fishing boats like
a broken rosary or promise, those
fog-bound shouts against the cliffs
still signaling wrong, wrong.
Sometimes I crave a faith simple
as my dog's who bides beside
the gate until his supper comes,
body and blood and joy in which
a master's absence is forgiven.

Beside these waters I am
learning signs to recite by heart,
what sea takes back cast up again:
shell, glass, stone, stick, worn
down to soft weed-wound
abstraction, the forms a human
soul might take through its
weddings and divorces of
energy and matter, waters
we come from and go back
to, that tread this earth awhile
in the temporal form of us.

Deschutes

Six deer file ahead of me
parting the sagebrush
as they pass, the youngest
barely free of its spots,
curious to understand
what possible danger I pose,
swiveling its ears to catch
the crunch of boots,
the slap of a fly line loosely
strung through guides,
the whisper of bird feathers
and, yes, deer hair in crude
approximation of a spent caddis.
Who knows what else they hear?
Now they turn and clatter
through shale, heading for
a rimrock where a vulture
rides the thermals.
So beautiful they are
I forget a moment to watch my step.

The river's note is wrong,
a soft whirring too close
to be water, too continuous
for one of those great gray
grasshoppers you always think
is what this is—a necklace of harm
sounding its dry, cautionary tail.
Around us, river, desert,
and the six deer seem to listen.
Where do you think you're going?—

less question than complaint from
one accustomed to his own way,
a crossroads bully cocked and ready.
I could bash its head in with a stone,
unholster a round to strike it blind.
Instead I wait, intent on fishing
the next riffle, if it will let me.
The trail is steep and narrow.
Gradually its sizzle subsides,
cooling in the desert's pan,
its tongue's Y probing the air
as if forgetful of what troubled it,
tension subsiding down its entire
length, its hammer head uncocked.
With a last *zzzt*, it gathers itself
into a ground squirrel's burrow
and disappears, like the vulture
over the rimrock and the six deer,
leaving me to myself.
Downstream, the trout can wait.

An Old Shirt of Raymond Carver's

For years now it's hung in a closet
with my other hunting and fishing shirts,
a faded thing I wouldn't be caught dead in.
Nor was he, though he wore it sometimes
when we fished the Strait, so I've kept it
safe from my wife's Goodwill recyclings.
How odd that a man's scent lives after him,
that twenty years later, I swear, I can
still catch the faint aroma of his sweat
and the cigarettes that killed him.

When I show it to my Lab he sniffs busily,
inspector dog, then cocks his head and looks
at me as if to ask, "Who's that?" If I said
"Fetch!" a cruel game to play on both of us,
he would circle aimlessly awhile, then go
and bring me one of his favorite toys,
goose, mallard, or that frayed Frisbee
I keep meaning to replace, the one he catches
without fail and always brings back to me.

Catch & Release

for Sir Francis Galton

How I love the meditative ritual of it,
laying line out over the water,
watching the fly drift through an eddy,
waiting for the splash, the tug and sizzle
of line leaving the reel, the bright silver
burst of a rainbow as it leaps.

Then the struggle, the careful giving
and taking until the trout lies spent
and gasping, the quick release,
the barbless hook slipped from its jaw.
No more painful, I tell myself, than
a dentist's needle, a lesson

in the need for selective feeding,
the fish held gently upright until
with a flick of its speckled tail
it disappears back into its current.
How I congratulate myself on my
skill, for teaching so many trout.

But once I caught the same fish
twice in one day, a distinctively
marked male impossible to mistake,
on a gray nymph in the early dawn
and, later in the afternoon, on a
size sixteen blue upright dry.

It wasn't its long hooked jaw
and flamboyant metallic pink
lateral stripe or the way its eye

tilted in its socket to look past me.
It was neither the homeliest
nor handsomest I'd caught.

But something I couldn't identify
made me reach past where it lay
catching its breath and waving
its pectorals as if to say goodbye
and sort through the gravel
until I found the right stone.

And the second time I killed it.
Natural selection I called it.
Let only the smartest survive.
But who was I fooling? *Eugenics*
the slippery word that escaped me.
And it's bothered me to this day.

Helium

In the shopping mall love is lighter than air,
the ceiling is full of hearts loose from their tethers.
One says *I love you!* another *Be my valentine!*
Outside, over the parking lot, two like blown kisses
or the promise of fidelity rise to separate heavens.

The checkout boy swears if I lose mine another
is free. Then why do I clutch the string so tightly,
juggling my groceries, unlocking the door?
My husband frowns into the evening news, *When
will we ever learn? Yes,* I want to echo, *When?*

Was it the news or another passing holiday,
the weather we discussed as if a weather change
might change us too? I wanted something else
for us, but instead of naming it, gave him a heart,
lighter than air, that will fly away if he lets it.

Dust

Where it cleared the roadway in a single bound,
a rabbit in its jaws, my fishing partner, stoned
on grass, watching the river for rising trout,
said *Deer*, having barely glimpsed it.
And I was fooled a second before I saw its spots,
the spontaneous brevity of its tail as it cleared
a ditch and disappeared among the boulders
tumbled from a distant rimrock. *Bobcat*, I said.

I had seen one in the wild before,
hunting with a friend, both of us bloodthirsty
teenagers, eager to shoot whatever
we could, both well practiced at picking
bumblebees off flowers with our .22s.
By the edge of a logging road it stretched
to sharpen claws against a stump, an easy shot.
But we jammed our rifles in our haste,
and in three puffs of dust it was down the road
and gone, an apparition of a cat, leaving only
its tracks to prove we'd seen it, puffs that eddy
as if it left them seconds ago, its bobcat
shape shifting to a speckled streak.

That's how you usually see them, in less than
a heartbeat, a privilege that catches you totally
by surprise, like a perfect rainbow rising
after you've cast for hours without luck—
of course you stand there with your jaw open
and forget to set the hook.
My wife frowns because wherever I have tried
to clean there still is dust—on the furniture

and countertops, the telephone, stereo and TV—
even the dog and cat are dusty as a dirt road.
I could swear I brushed them spotless. She has
never hunted, yet tracks us by the spots we leave.
Sometimes she misses the life she left where
everything was clearer, or at least cleaner,
misses her parents' Shepherd, who snatches bees
like pollen-speckled peppers from the lavender
beside her parents' deck, misses the view
everywhere you turn of mountains.
Here, the houses hem us in, and the dailiness
of dust that settles in the wake of strokes
that will never come clean enough
till we are quit of this untidy world, become
the thing we spent a lifetime wiping out.
How can I convince her that happiness is a bobcat,
and where the bobcat's been, the dust still hangs.

Mary

When her plane went down over Iowa one afternoon
I had no idea; only years later, after a friend told me,
I had to imagine those final moments, the Grumman
boxed in by heavy cumulus, the lightning cracking down,
and she and her husband fighting the controls, trying
every trick they knew to save themselves and failing.

A year earlier she had phoned long distance when I was out
but left no number where I could reach her,
only a message about being unhappy and needing to talk.
In the years since I have often thought of her
and blamed myself for not trying harder to reach her,
and I have also thought of that telephone call
I might have answered telling her to leave her husband
and fly west instead to me—to think I might have saved her.

But then I catch myself in another of my old lies, knowing
I would have listened to her troubles instead, as friends
and sometimes old lovers do, and offered nothing but
my sympathy, a bit of gossip about my wife and daughter,
upheld like the miles of mountains between us.

Silver Thaw

One by one the glass trees
   break, the streets empty
and the power out.
   No one dares step outside.
Waking an hour ago
   we discovered this brittle,
beautiful world.

Limbs of our Norway maple
   glitter and sag dangerously.
Tree I have nurtured and shaped,
   why do they call it a silver thaw
when everything is frozen?

Another limb cracks.
   The crystals ricochet,
tinkling over the street's ice,
   the promise of trees broken.

After the freeze is over,
   After the linesmen have cut
and hauled away the fallen,
   will the ones remaining
regain their former grace
   before it's our turn to join
those that have gone?

It comforted me to think
   that after I die
this tree would still be here.
   Now I'm uncertain, afraid

it might go the way of the
   homes I have lived in, some
razed for urban renewal,
   and two, like my high school,
burned to the ground,
   victims of bad heating
bad wiring, my stepfather's
   home improvements.

Once we believed in a war
   to end all wars, an aftermath
of everlasting peace,
   but we were wrong.
Before he died, Jack
   said, "It's a good thing we
don't live to be two hundred.
   A man can't stand that
much change."
   And Jon's comment,
"People don't change much,"
   closer to the mark.
Charon's coin and the
   Buddhist's belief that
when we die all is remembered
   and as quickly forgotten.
Rings of water from a dropped
   stone, growth rings in the
core of a tree, everything
   that was, is, not.

Talk Show

The man who has never cheated on his wife is outraged
at their infidelities. *This isn't love!* he screams. *How in*
God's name can they live with themselves? It has not yet
occurred to him how the thought that we are blameless
must leave us lonely, estranged from that great fellowship
of the damned. *If I thought the majority of my fellow*
human beings were condemned to hell it would be
my moral duty to join them, another guest answers.
But the man who is outraged is still outraged, and somewhere
the woman he will leave his wife and children for
is putting down her glass, touching her hair, already moving
toward him, though neither knows it yet.
For now, though they exist apart in space and time and one
or both live that oldest of lies, the presumption of innocence,
the gears that govern everything are moving them toward
each other, precise as figures on a clock, one with conviction
aimed like a sword, the other, disarming as she is alarming
on the hour, their hour, she lifts her perfect hand as if to bless.

"The Secret of Poetry is Cruelty"
Jon Anderson, 1940-2007

It was a line I kicked against when you first wrote it,
unwilling as others to accept the cruel truth of it,
the many failures for each small success,
the wrong we do others in the name of art.
You desired, always, to be wise beyond your years,
confusing that with acting old before your time.
Time the affliction you could live without,
if in one awful breath you could bear witness
against us, against yourself, the "lips of the poor"
a huge, declamatory petal opening, demanding
our self-annihilating kiss, "the campaign for peace
in our time" degenerating to "the coffee talk of saints."
And someone's unkind remark you believed
had "hurt the land." What answer could you give it
finally but your own silence, knowing you would
be missed, knowing how much, in reading you,
we would miss, if only you could become what you
most loved, a scene in someone's "guarded biography,"
the last trace of himself erased.

First and Last

Often he followed tracks only to find
a pile of entrails and four legs,
proof of someone else's triumph,
a winter's worth of meat in the freezer,
and maybe a trophy head on the wall.
Until that day it was his turn,
and he saw, as from a vision,
the huge tree of its head branching
from behind a clump of evergreen,
a moment he'd so often practiced for
the rifle seemed to aim and fire itself.
Had he missed? Only the bracken
trembling, a distant raven's bell-like
croak heard dimly through falling flakes
before the elk's knees buckled
and it pitched snout-first into snow.
And as he stepped closer, the deep
whistle and vapor of its last breath,
its body bulging out of the drift
like a rucked-up brown and beige rug.

Afterwards he would never tell
of that crazy urge to dance
and smear his face with blood,
or of the remorse that follows
even the cleanest kill, the clarity
when he noticed, as never before,
the bone gray alders jeweled
with ice, and he was certain
he could feel its spirit escaping
from that life he had stolen

as surely as if it had just slipped
into the trees and disappeared.
The meat he would eat that winter
was strong with the taste of it.

If to hunt curiously exposes an ache
for more life—our own—as Hemingway
supposed, this is a story
he might tell his grandchildren.

Behind him its lifeless fake eyes
reflect firelight from the wall
as though its wintery antlers
branched from his own head,
as if the animal he had spent
a lifetime hunting had come at last
to rest in the leather chair snoring
over a chapter finished
in a book fallen to the floor.

Nature

My wife can't stand those programs where something
is killing something else. And who can blame her?
It's nature, I tell her, as if that made a difference.
The death of the least furred thing brings her to tears,
as if she were responsible and might prevent it.

The cheetah streaks after a Thompson's gazelle,
trips it and seizes it by the throat. A mother wildebeest
tries in vain to save its calf from a pack of hyenas.
And Genevieve turns her head from this carnage,
angry because I go on watching night after night,

the Serengeti, Sarajevo, trying to sort out the difference
between the lion that kills a cheetah's cubs and leaves
them to rot, and a sniper's estimate of the distance
between himself and a mother out gathering wood.
I know I should try harder to shield my wife from what

she cannot bear, and yet some streak of yellow-eyed
watchfulness instructs me to wait and do nothing,
like the scientist who will not interfere because nature,
as he perceives it, condemns the weak to inherit nothing.
Once, a harder-minded woman scoffed when

I broke up a fight between two stupid mallards bent
on murder, or so it seemed to me, the air full of down.
It must have looked silly, a man in up to his knees,
shouting at ducks, so I didn't blame her for laughing.
But let me always right the beetle struggling on its back,

stand between the dog and cat and the cat and sparrow,
foolish and impractical as she accused me of being.
And let me remember also why I married Genevieve.
Because she is kind and will not accept what others take
for granted: that nature is otherwise and man no better.

Ode to the John Day

for David James Duncan and Bill Bakke

Near this place I wanted to fish
they dug up Mammoth fossils
from an age deeper than I can imagine,
from volcanic, sage-brushed slopes
where families awoke to break the dawn
with others of their kind wearing
nothing but skin, brief hunter-gatherers
driven out of time, where occasional owls
still patrol the moused acres of grain
along the valley floor, beside this river
named after an early settler,
winding and ripening to its end.

Here, a little closer to its source,
the water meanders, riffled by an upthrust
geology too recent to be polished flat,
not yet removed from its wilder state,
despite the bleat of animal to automobile,
the gridwork of wire sprinkling
occasional sodium vapor lights,
and the stars come out on earth,
a tamer congregation from older celestial
orbits too bright to harbor only us.

Years before the first white ranchers
settled this valley a fringe of trees
shaded the river's edge,
a place for insects' airy quadrilles
above cool shadowy waters,
haven for Dolly Varden and steelhead,
its shallows truculent

with spawning salmon.
       Then came mining dredges,
a stampede of hooves along
              soon-to-be-denuded river margins,
brown with tumbled spoil.
       The paths we tramp are narrower here,
through overgrazed hills
              terraced by sheep and cattle,
but the river's subversive whisper
              persists that what was broken
can still mend.

       Here on the John Day, I praise one
who acted on his own to fence away the herds
              that trample everything to dust.
His river reach blooms with new green growth,
              a promise of trees and clearer water
for the last survivors of once great runs,
              and here and there a song starts up,
meadowlark or mourning dove,
              one note, then another, become
a chorus as heaven's light breaks
              in the mind
of every waking thing.
       I think of grass beginning
to sprout between wire and river,
              harbinger of trees and eventual shade,
this guardian net for steelhead and salmon
              on their way home,
this steel-thorned fretwork
              the wind leaps through.

Some previous titles in the Carnegie Mellon Poetry Series

2013

Oregon, Henry Carlile

Selvage, Donna Johnson

At the Autopsy of Vaslav Nijinksy, Bridget Lowe

Silvertone, Dzivinia Orlowsky

Fibonacci Batman: New & Selected Poems (1991-2011),
        Maureen Seaton

When We Were Cherished, Eve Shelnutt

The Fortunate Era, Arthur Smith

Birds of the Air, David Yezzi

2012

Now Make an Altar, Amy Beeder

Still Some Cake, James Cummins

Comet Scar, James Harms

Early Creatures, Native Gods, K. A. Hays

That Was Oasis, Michael McFee

Blue Rust, Joseph Millar

Spitshine, Anne Marie Rooney

Civil Twilight, Margot Schilpp

2011

Having a Little Talk with Capital P Poetry, Jim Daniels

Oz, Nancy Eimers

Working in Flour, Jeff Friedman

Scorpio Rising: Selected Poems, Richard Katrovas

The Politics, Benjamin Paloff

Copperhead, Rachel Richardson

2010

The Diminishing House, Nicky Beer

A World Remembered, T. Alan Broughton
Say Sand, Daniel Coudriet
Knock Knock, Heather Hartley
In the Land We Imagined Ourselves, Jonathan Johnson
Selected Early Poems: 1958-1983, Greg Kuzma
The Other Life: Selected Poems, Herbert Scott
Admission, Jerry Williams

2009
Divine Margins, Peter Cooley
Cultural Studies, Kevin A. González
Dear Apocalypse, K. A. Hays
Warhol-o-rama, Peter Oresick
Cave of the Yellow Volkswagen, Maureen Seaton
Group Portrait from Hell, David Schloss
Birdwatching in Wartime, Jeffrey Thomson

2008
The Grace of Necessity, Samuel Green
After West, James Harms
Anticipate the Coming Reservoir, John Hoppenthaler
Convertible Night, Flurry of Stones, Dzvinia Orlowsky
Parable Hunter, Ricardo Pau-Llosa
The Book of Sleep, Eleanor Stanford

2007
Trick Pear, Suzanne Cleary
So I Will Till the Ground, Gregory Djanikian
Black Threads, Jeff Friedman
Drift and Pulse, Kathleen Halme
The Playhouse Near Dark, Elizabeth Holmes

On the Vanishing of Large Creatures, Susan Hutton
One Season Behind, Sarah Rosenblatt
Indeed I Was Pleased with the World, Mary Ruefle
The Situation, John Skoyles

2006
Burn the Field, Amy Beeder
The Sadness of Others, Hayan Charara
A Grammar to Waking, Nancy Eimers
Dog Star Delicatessen: New and Selected Poems 1979–2006,
        Mekeel McBride
Shinemaster, Michael McFee
Eastern Mountain Time, Joyce Peseroff
Dragging the Lake, Robert Thomas

2005
Things I Can't Tell You, Michael Dennis Browne
Bent to the Earth, Blas Manuel De Luna
Blindsight, Carol Hamilton
Fallen from a Chariot, Kevin Prufer
Needlegrass, Dennis Sampson
Laws of My Nature, Margot Schilpp
Sleeping Woman, Herbert Scott
Renovation, Jeffrey Thomson

2004
The Women Who Loved Elvis All Their Lives, Fleda Brown
The Chronic Liar Buys a Canary, Elizabeth Edwards
Freeways and Aqueducts, James Harms
Prague Winter, Richard Katrovas
Trains in Winter, Jay Meek

Tristimania, Mary Ruefle

Venus Examines Her Breast, Maureen Seaton

Various Orbits, Thom Ward

2003

Trouble, Mary Baine Campbell

A Place Made of Starlight, Peter Cooley

Taking Down the Angel, Jeff Friedman

Lives of Water, John Hoppenthaler

Imitation of Life, Allison Joseph

Except for One Obscene Brushstroke, Dzvinia Orlowsky

The Mastery Impulse, Ricardo Pau-Llosa

Casino of the Sun, Jerry Williams

2002

Keeping Time, Suzanne Cleary

Astronaut, Brian Henry

What it Wasn't, Laura Kasischke

Slow Risen Among the Smoke Trees, Elizabeth Kirschner

The Finger Bone, Kevin Prufer

Among the Musk Ox People, Mary Ruefle

The Late World, Arthur Smith

2001

Day Moon, Jon Anderson

The Origin of Green, T. Alan Broughton

Lovers in the Used World, Gillian Conoley

Quarters, James Harms

Mastodon, 80% Complete, Jonathan Johnson

The Deepest Part of the River, Mekeel McBride

Earthly, Michael McFee

Ten Thousand Good Mornings, James Reiss
The World's Last Night, Margot Schilpp
Sex Lives of the Poor and Obscure, David Schloss
Glacier Wine, Maura Stanton
Voyages in English, Dara Wier

2000
Blue Jesus, Jim Daniels
Years Later, Gregory Djanikian
Winter Morning Walks: 100 Postcards to Jim Harrison, Ted Kooser
Mortal Education, Joyce Peseroff
How Things Are, James Richardson
On the Waterbed They Sank to Their Own Levels, Sarah Rosenblatt
Post Meridian, Mary Ruefle
Constant Longing, Dennis Sampson
Hierarchies of Rue, Roger Sauls
Small Boat with Oars of Different Size, Thom Ward